Developing Literacy Skills

Through History

KEY STAGE 1: Y1–2

CHRISTINE MOORCROFT

HOPSCOTCH

A division of MA Education Ltd

◆ Contents ◆

Published by Hopscotch, A division of MA Education Ltd
St Jude's Church, Dulwich Road, Herne Hill, London SE24 0PB
Tel: 020 7738 5454

© 2008 MA Education Ltd

Written by Christine Moorcroft
Series design by Blade Communications
Illustrated by Cathy Gilligan
Cover illustrated by Susan Hutchison
Printed in the UK by CLE

Christine Moorcroft hereby asserts her moral right to be identified as the author of this work in accordance with the Copyright, Designs and Patents Act 1988.

ISBN 978-1-90223-975-0

Literacy through history

Introduction

ABOUT THE SERIES

Developing Literacy Skills Through History is a series of books aimed at developing key literacy skills using a range of written genres based on a history theme, from Key Stage 1 through to Key Stage 2.

The series offers a structured approach which provides detailed lesson plans to teach specific literacy and history skills. A unique feature of the series is the provision of differentiated photocopiable activities aimed at considerably reducing teacher preparation time. Suggestions for follow-up activities for both literacy and history ensure maximum use of this resource.

ABOUT THIS BOOK

This book is for teachers of children at Key Stage 1, Years 1–2 and Scottish levels P1–3. It aims to:

◆ develop children's literacy and history skills through exposure to and experience of a range of stimulating texts with supporting differentiated activities which are both diversified and challenging
◆ support teachers by providing practical teaching methods based on whole-class, group, paired and individual teaching
◆ encourage enjoyment and curiosity as well as develop skills of interpretation and response.

CHAPTER CONTENT

Literacy objectives

This outlines the aims for the literacy activities suggested in the lesson plan.

History objectives

This outlines the history learning objectives that relate to the lesson plan.

Resources

This lists the different resources that the teacher needs to teach the lesson.

Starting point: Whole class

This provides ideas for introducing the activity and may include key questions to ask the children.

Using the photocopiable text

This explains how to use the provided text extract with the children as a shared reading activity and introduction to the group work. It may also be used by groups during the group work.

Group activities

This explains how to use each sheet as well as providing guidance on the level of attainment of the children who will benefit most from each sheet.

Plenary session

This suggests ideas for whole-class sessions to discuss the learning outcomes and follow-up work.

Follow-up ideas for literacy

This contains suggestions for further literacy activities related to the lesson plan, which can be carried out at another time.

Follow up ideas for history

This contains suggestions for further history activities which might be carried out at another time or during a designated history lesson.

Talking about the past

Literacy objectives

✦ To read and write captions and labels. (Y1, T1: T12, T14)
✦ To write names using initial capitals. (Y1, T2: S7)
✦ To identify separate phonemes within words. (Y1, T2: W3)

History objectives

(Unit 1)
✦ To talk about past events in the children's families, using words connected with time.
✦ To put events in own families in chronological order.

Resources

✦ Photographs brought in by you, the children or adult helpers, of family events such as birthdays, weddings, naming ceremonies and baptisms.

Starting point: Whole class

✦ Show the children two enlarged photographs of an event in your own family: one from before you were born and one that includes yourself when younger. How can the children tell that the pictures show special events? They might notice the clothes people are wearing or 'special occasion' items such as flowers. What kind of event was each one? Challenge the children to identify you in the second photograph. Ask them if they think each event took place recently or a long time ago. How can they tell? Introduce vocabulary connected with chronology: 'a few weeks ago', 'a few months ago', 'a few years ago', 'many years ago', 'before I was born'.

✦ Ask the children on what special occasions they have had family photographs taken. Help them to explain when the events took place, using the vocabulary you have already introduced.

Using the photocopiable text

✦ Photocopy and enlarge the text 'Who's that?' on page 6. Tell the children that it is a story about a photograph of a special occasion in a family. Read the story while the children follow it. Point to the appropriate character in the picture as you read each 'Who's that?' The children should be able to join in Jake's response 'It can't be! ...'s grown up. That's a little boy (or girl)'.

✦ After reading the story, ask the children for what kind of special event the picture was taken. Encourage them to explain why Jake does not recognise his uncles and aunties and some of the adults. Why do they look like children? Use the phrases 'before Jake was born' and 'when his mum was a little girl'.

✦ Ask the children to take turns to point out a person's name in the story. How can they tell it is a name? Point out the capital letter. Write the names on the board. As the children tell you the names point to the capital letters again. When else do we use capital letters? Ask the children to find them at the beginning of sentences. Remind them about full stops.

✦ Point out the labels on the picture and model how to label a family picture (perhaps using an enlarged version of one brought in by you or one of the children). Together, write some captions to go with the photograph in sentence form. Remind the children about capital letters and full stops.

✦ Tell the children that they are now going to label a family picture.

Group activities

Using the differentiated activity sheets

Activity sheet 1: This is for children who need more support with writing labels. They are required to label some people on a wedding photograph similar to the one in the story. They should refer to the picture and labels on page 6.

Activity sheet 2: This is for children who can read simple sentences and write captions. They are asked to write captions consisting of simple sentences that begin 'This is ...' They should refer to the picture and labels on page 6.

Activity sheet 3: This is for children who can read and write independently and can write sentences. They are asked to write sentences about people in the 'wedding photograph' in the story on page 6 that show that the wedding took place before Jake was born.

Talking about the past

 Plenary session

Display an enlarged copy of the 'wedding photograph' on page 6, with the people's names masked. Invite the children who completed Activity sheet 1 to write the names in the gaps (using their own copies for reference). Invite the children who did Activity sheet 2 to supply a sentence about selected people in the picture as you point to them.

Write some of their sentences on the board (without the capital letters and full stops) and ask the children to check that they are correct. Invite the children who did Activity sheet 3 to supply sentences about selected people that show that the wedding took place before Jake was born. The children could check their own work for capital letters and full stops.

 Follow-up ideas for literacy

♦ Talk about the way in which Jake read the word 'wedding', which he did not know. Are there any other words in the story that were new to the children? Which others can be read by sounding out the phonemes? Which names can be read in this way?

♦ Identify any new words whose phonemes cannot be sounded. Point out any letter strings in them that the children might know. For example, 'an', 'if' and 'it'.

♦ Look at the questions in the text, particularly the first words. Talk about other words that are often used at the beginnings of questions, such as 'When'

and 'Why'. The children could bring in photographs and write questions to which they would like to find the answers from other children's photographs.

♦ Look at the words spoken by Jake and his gran. Invite two children to enact the roles of Jake and his gran. The children could then look for speech marks in the text of the story and identify the words that were spoken. They could go on to make up a role play about an event in their own family.

♦ Ask the children to make up stories, modelled on this one, about photographs of events in their own families. Their stories could be put together to make a class book entitled 'Events in our families'.

 Follow-up ideas for history

♦ The children could tell the rest of their class or group the story of an event in their family's past using a photograph they have brought in. Do they know who the people are? Do they look different now? Why?

♦ Ask the children if the event was a long time ago. Introduce or remind the children of words and phrases such as 'before I was born', 'before you were born', 'last year', 'ten years ago', 'when Mum was a little girl', 'when Grandad was a boy', 'recently', 'before Christmas', '1950s', '1960s', '1970s'.

♦ Show the children a photograph of a very recent wedding and one which took place 30 to 50 years ago. (Have both pictures in colour or both in black and white, since children sometimes assume that a black and white photograph is old). Explain

how long ago the pictures were taken, using the words introduced above. How can the children tell which is the old and which is the new picture? Draw their attention to the clothes and hairstyles. What differences do they notice?

♦ Encourage the children to bring to school pictures of weddings or other family events from different generations. Encourage them to complete charts for comparing the photographs.

♦ Read with the children (and encourage them to read for themselves) fiction books about the passage of time in families, for example, *Grandma's Bill* by Jane Jonson (Macdonald, 1990), *Once There Were Giants* by Martin Waddell (Walker, 1989), *The Patchwork Quilt* by Valerie Flournoy (Puffin, 1998) and *From Me To You* by Paul Rogers (Orchard, 1987).

Who's that?

A big white book lay on Gran's table. On the front was one word written in curly silver letters: 'Wedding'.

Jake sounded out all the letters, 'W–e–dd–i–n–g, Wedding!'

'That's right – Wedding. Look at the photographs if you like,' said Gran.

The photographs were fixed on to pieces of stiff white card which had a ripply, bumpy feel and silver edges. Each page had a silver squiggle in the corner. Over each page was a piece of white tissue paper.

Jake lifted the tissue and wondered whose wedding it was. He thought he knew some of the people, but he wasn't quite sure. One photograph showed a lot of people with the bride and groom –

Mum and Dad! They looked different – sort of smooth and shiny. So did Gran, Grandad, Nana and Grandpa.

'Who's that?' asked Jake, pointing to a little girl next to Grandad.

'That's Auntie May,' said Gran.

'It can't be! That's a little girl!'

'Auntie May was only six then,' said Gran.

'Who's that?' asked Jake, pointing to a little boy in front of Grandpa.

'That's Ben.'

'It can't be! That's a little boy!'

'Ben was only five then,' said Gran.

And so Gran told Jake who all the people were. He did know them, but they all looked so different!

✦ Family events ✦

✦ Write a name under each picture.
✦ Use the words at the bottom of the page to help you.

Uncle	Tom	Mum	Dad
Ben	Auntie	May	Rani

Photocopiable

✦ Family events ✦

✦ Write the missing words in the sentences.
✦ Read the sentences.

This is _____

She was _____

This is _____

He was _____

This is _____

He was _____

This is _____

She was _____

| Rani | Ben | Auntie May |
| Uncle Tom | a little girl | a little boy |

◆ Family events ◆

✦ Write a caption for each person below from the wedding picture.
✦ Read the captions.

_____

_____

_____

_____

_____

_____

...

Toys from the past

Literacy objectives

◆ To write labels for drawings. (Y1, T2: T22)
◆ To write simple sentences, rereading them and recognising whether or not they make sense. (Y1, T1: S4)

History objectives

(Unit 1)
◆ To identify similarities and differences between old toys and modern toys.
◆ To describe the characteristics of old and new objects.
◆ To communicate what they have learned about toys.

Resources

◆ A collection of old and modern toys.
◆ Pictures of old and modern toys.

Starting point: Whole class

◆ Show the children a collection of old and modern toys and invite them to choose a toy to talk about. Ask them to describe the toy (orally), name it, talk about any important parts of it and say how they would use it. Encourage them to say who would play with the toy (a child of their own age, older, a bit younger or a baby), and whether the child would play with it alone or with a brother, sister or friend. Is it an old toy or a modern toy? How can they tell? They could look for wear and tear, but also point out other clues, for example computer toys are a modern invention. The children might not be aware that electricity, batteries and materials such as plastic and nylon were available when their parents, and even some of their grandparents, were young. Tell them that these materials were not used in very old toys (before the childhood of their grandparents).

◆ Write the names of the toys on labels, mix them up and ask the children to help you to match them to the toys.

◆ Write two labels, 'Old toys' and 'Modern toys'. Hold up the toys one at a time and ask the children to which set they belong. How can they tell?

Using the photocopiable text

◆ Photocopy and enlarge the text 'Mary's toys' on page 12. Tell the children that they are going to hear about a woman who shows a class of children some of her old toys and tells them about how she played with her toys. Read the text while the children follow it. Point to the appropriate toys in the pictures as you read about them. Discuss vocabulary that might be new to them, for example 'whip', 'lash', 'stud' and 'frame'.

◆ Invite the children to talk about tops they have used. In what ways were they similar to, and different from, Mary's top? Notice that all tops spin, but that there are different ways of making them spin. Ask them to talk about the materials from which tops are made. Encourage them to use technical vocabulary for the parts of a top.

◆ Ask the children how Mary's roller skates are similar to, and different from, modern roller blades. Talk about the materials used and the style of the skates and roller blades. Encourage them to use technical vocabulary for the parts of roller skates and roller blades.

◆ Choose a toy from the collection as a model. Draw a quick sketch of it on the board and then agree words that could be used to label it. Then ask the children to tell you some sentences they could write about the toy. Revise sentences, capital letters and full stops. Ask them how they can be sure that a sentence makes sense. Remind them how important it is to reread their sentences.

Group activities

Using the differentiated activity sheets

Activity sheet 1: This is for children who can recognise the initial sound of a word and the letter or letters by which it can be represented in writing. They are beginning to recognise critical features of words (their shape and length). They can copy words letter by letter.

Activity sheet 2: This is for children who can recognise the initial sound of a word and the letter or letters by which it can be represented in writing. They are learning to find words by their first letter in an alphabetical list. They can recognise critical features of words (their shape and length)

Toys from the past

and can copy words. They are developing an understanding of sentences and are beginning to recognise a sentence.

Activity sheet 3: This is for children who can recognise the initial sound of a word and the letter or letters by which it can be represented in writing, and can find the word in an alphabetical list. They can recognise critical features of words (their shape and length) and can copy words. They understand what a sentence is, can identify sentences in text and are beginning to write their own sentences.

 Plenary session

+ Display an enlarged copy of the toy from the activity sheets and invite the children who completed Activity sheet 1 to write the words in the gaps (using their own copies for reference). Invite those who worked on Activity sheet 2 to supply a sentence about how each part of the toy works. Ask the others to check that it is a sentence and to correct it if necessary. Invite the children who did Activity sheet 3 to read out some of their sentences about how to use the toy.

 Follow-up ideas for literacy

+ Encourage the children to bring in toys and draw labelled pictures of them, referring to prepared word banks. Some children could write sentences about their toys, saying what they are made of and how they work. Their work could be presented in a class book about toys. Challenge the children to make personal collections of words for parts of toys and contribute to a class word bank about toys. This could be organised by fixing a long strip of paper horizontally to a display board which the children can reach. With the children's help write the letters of the alphabet along the strip of paper and ask them to write their words beneath the correct letter.

+ To help the children to recognise the words for parts of toys, you could make a table-top display of toys and write labels for parts of them. During plenary sessions, the children could read out the words on the labels and match them to the words in the word bank.

+ Ask the children to demonstrate and describe how a toy works. Help them to write simple instructions for using it. Their instructions could be in the form of annotated drawings.

 Follow-up ideas for history

+ Ask the children to sort collections of objects into 'old' and 'new'. Talk about the characteristics of each set, encouraging the children to use adjectives such as 'shiny', 'rusty', 'dented', 'bent', 'dirty' and 'clean'. Write these adjectives on cards, display the cards and discuss what they mean. Ask the children to match the words to the objects. Are all dirty, broken or rusty objects old? Are all shiny, clean objects new?

+ You could help the children to make a class toy museum. Talk about how the toys could be grouped, for example by age or by type (outdoor and indoor); toys for playing alone and toys for playing with a friend; toys which move, toys which make a noise,

toys to use for making things, and board games. Ask the children to write labels for the exhibits.

+ The museum could be used for role-play. Encourage the children to make signs ('Entrance', opening times, admission charges, direction signs and so on) and to show visitors from other classes around the museum.

+ Invite the children to arrange toys of the same type along a timeline, for example they could arrange teddy bears, roller skates, roller boots and roller blades, board games, battery-operated toys, cars and trains from 'old' to 'new'.

Indoor toys were only for rainy days. We played outside most of the time – in the school playground, in the park and in the road where we lived. Few people had a car in the 1950s, so the roads were much safer.

My favourite toy was a top and whip. The whip had a wooden handle with a thin leather lash. Cheaper ones had a lash made of string. Leather was much better for whipping the top to make it spin. This is how I made the top spin.

To keep the top spinning we whipped it. The top was made from wood, with a metal stud at the bottom. I used to chalk patterns on the flat part at the top of it. The colours mixed as the top spun. Sometimes I glued pieces of silver paper or gummed shapes on to the top.

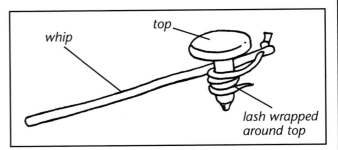

whip
top
lash wrapped around top

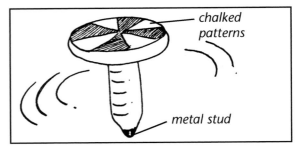

chalked patterns
metal stud

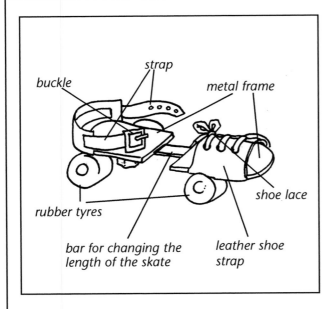

strap
buckle
metal frame
shoe lace
rubber tyres
bar for changing the length of the skate
leather shoe strap

Roller skates were not like modern roller blades. They were made of steel with rubber tyres on the wheels. The skates had leather straps with laces which we fastened over our shoes. Underneath the skates there was a big metal nut which you could loosen with a spanner to alter the length of the skates. We did not need to buy new ones when our feet grew. I was always falling over and cutting my knees and elbows. We didn't have knee and elbow pads.

Photocopiable

◆ Labels ◆

◆ Write the words on the labels.

handle   bulb   colour filter dial
'on' and 'off' switch

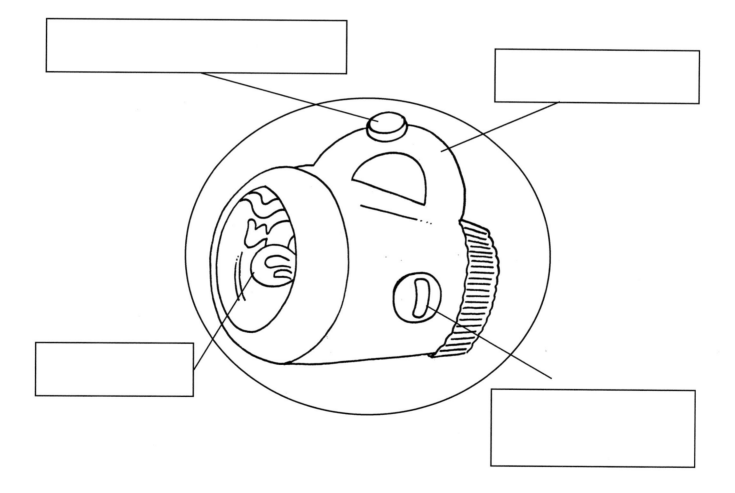

◆ Now draw a line to where you think the batteries are and write the label.

◆ Labels ◆

◆ Write the words on the labels.

handle	bulb	'on' and 'off' switch	colour filter dial

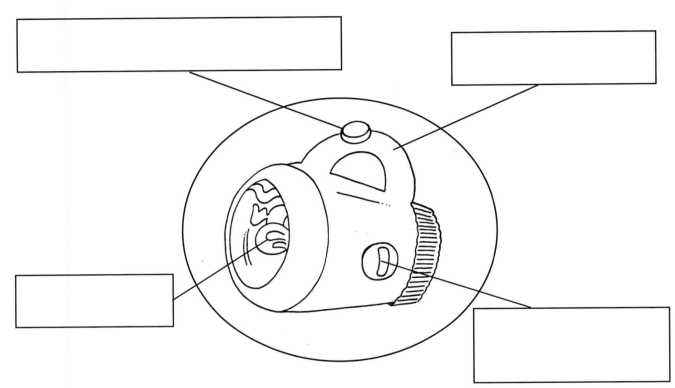

◆ Draw a line to where you think the batteries are and write the label.

◆ Now complete these sentences to say what each part is for.

1 The b_____ give the torch power.

2 The b_____ is the light.

4 The c_____ f_____ d_____ makes the light green.

5 You hold the torch by the h_____ .

6 The 'o____' and 'o____' switch makes it go on and off.

◆ L a b e l s ◆

◆ Write the words on the labels.

handle	bulb	'on' and 'off' switch	colour filter dial

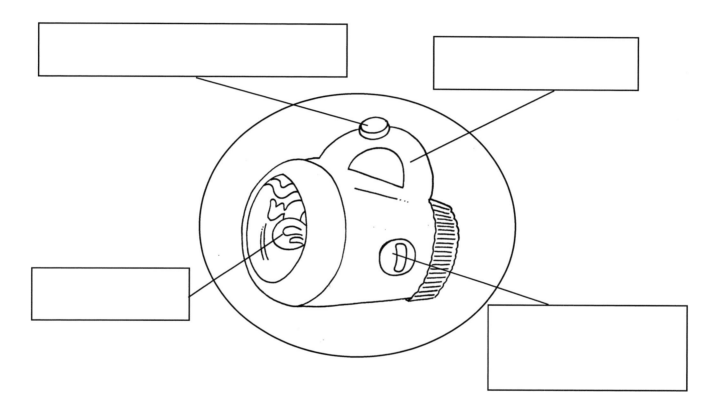

◆ Draw a line to where you think the batteries are and write the label.

◆ Now write some sentences about how to use the toy.

> Use a dictionary.

_____

_____

_____

_____

_____

Chapter 3

Clothes from the past

Literacy objectives

✦ To practise and secure alphabetical letter knowledge. (Y1, T1: W2)
✦ To make personal collections of significant words linked to topics. (Y1, T1: W12)

History objectives

(Unit 2)
✦ To learn about the past beyond living memory.
✦ To use pictures to learn about the past.

Resources

✦ Portrait paintings, drawings and photographs of children from all classes of society from the second half of the nineteenth century, for example *Many Happy Returns of the Day* (William Frith, Harrogate Museum & Gallery), *The Pinch of Poverty* (T B Kennington, Thomas Coram Foundation), *The Lowther Arcade* (H C Bryant, Coutts & Co) and *Blind Man's Buff* (George Goodwin Kilburne, The Priory Gallery, Cheltenham).
✦ A collection of children's indoor and outdoor clothing.

Starting point: Whole class

✦ Show the children pictures of Victorian children and ask them to compare their own clothes with those in the pictures. If possible, show them pictures of boys wearing dresses. Explain that boys wore dresses until they were about five years old. Boys older than that from poor families sometimes wore their elder sisters' cast-off clothes.

✦ The children could sort the pictures into two sets: rich children and poor children. Ask them how they can tell to which group the children belong.

✦ Talk about the fastenings on the children's own clothing. Ask them to name the different types of fastenings on their indoor and outdoor clothing, and write the words on the board, for example 'button', 'zip', 'buckle', 'Velcro' and 'laces'. Point out the fastenings of the children's clothing in the pictures and invite the children to compare them with those on their own clothes.

✦ Read the manufacturer's labels on a collection of clothing and draw attention to the materials. Tell the children which ones are modern materials and which ones were also used a long time ago.

Using the photocopiable text

✦ Before the activity, write the letters of the alphabet on separate sheets of paper and fix them (in order) on to a display board, or write the letters (in order) in separate boxes on a chalkboard or wipe-off board.

✦ Photocopy and enlarge the text 'Getting dressed a long time ago' on page 18. Tell the children they are going to hear about about a boy and girl from a long time ago getting dressed. Read the recounts while the children follow them. Highlight any words that might be new to them or that they might not be able to read. Write the words on the board. Circle the initial letters of those words and point them out to the children. Write these words underneath the correct letters in the alphabet on the board. Then model how to find them in a dictionary. Reread the new words and encourage the children to repeat them; they can enjoy the sounds of words such as 'chemise', 'breeches' and 'drawers'.

✦ Invite the children to come out and name an item of clothing they are wearing. Ask the others with which letter the word begins, and help them to write the word beneath the appropriate letter.

Group activities

Using the differentiated activity sheets

Activity sheet 1: This is for children who can recognise the initial letter of a word and match it to its counterpart in an alphabet. They need to know the names of the letters and understand alphabetical order. They are beginning to recognise the alphabetical order of a list in which not all the letters of the alphabet appear. They are developing an understanding of how dictionaries are organised.

Activity sheet 2: This is for children who can recognise the initial letter of a word. They need to have a secure knowledge of the alphabet and can arrange letters in alphabetical order even when some letters are missing. They are learning to arrange words in alphabetical order by first letter only. They understand how dictionaries are organised and are beginning to use them in their work.

Clothes from the past

Activity sheet 3: This is for children who can recognise the initial letter of a word. They need to have a secure knowledge of the alphabet and can arrange letters in alphabetical order with some letters missing, and words in alphabetical order by first letter only. They understand how dictionaries are organised, can use them in their work and are developing skills in using alphabetical order to organise their own work.

◆ *Plenary session*

◆ Display an enlarged copy of Activity sheet 3. Go round the class identifying the names of different pieces of clothing and write them on the board. Circle all the initial letters and then agree which of these initial letters appear on the enlarged copy of Activity sheet 3. Those that do can be written on the sheet. You might like to ask some of the children to come up and write them in.

◆ If there are spaces on the sheet, can the children think of items of clothes that begin with this initial letter and write the words for them in the correct place?

◆ *Follow-up ideas for literacy*

◆ Challenge the children to make a class dictionary or word bank of clothes, arranged in alphabetical order. Provide a book with a letter of the alphabet on each page. This could be developed as a 'clothes fact-file' in which the letters could be written on the tabs of index cards. The children draw, label and write about a piece of clothing on a card and then insert it into the correct section of the fact-file. This could be about present-day clothing or clothing from a long time ago.

◆ Ask the children to write their own recounts of getting dressed, based on those of Henry and Alice. Encourage them to use words that indicate the passage of time, such as 'first', 'then', 'next' and 'after that', and to vary the words they use, so that there is no repetition of 'and then ... and then ...'. Some children might find it easier to draw their clothes (or arrange pictures of clothes cut from catalogues) in the order they put them on, and then label them. Others could do this and add captions, such as 'I put on my shirt'.

◆ *Follow-up ideas for history*

◆ Take the children to a museum in which they can look at Victorian clothing, or provide examples of Victorian clothing (or replicas) for them to examine, or even put on, in the classroom. Tell them the names of materials used often then (but seldom nowadays) for making children's clothes – for example, taffeta, velvet, linen and muslin. Provide samples of the materials which the children can handle and wash to compare them with modern fabrics such as nylon and polyester. Talk about 'easy-care fabrics' and tell them that a long time ago people did not wash their clothes (or themselves) as often as they do nowadays and that there were no dry-cleaners.

◆ Ask the children to collect pictures of fashionable clothes such as tracksuits and trainers. Talk about why some people like to wear particular brands or styles. Encourage them to find out about children's fashions from a long time ago by looking at pictures which include boys dressed in sailor suits and girls wearing frilly dresses.

Henry

Henry wore a long, loose shirt made of white cotton. He tucked it into his woollen breeches. His breeches were trousers which came down to just below his knees. His knees did not show because his woollen stockings came up over his knees. He wore leather boots with laces. They came up over the ankle and up to the calf.

Before he went out Henry put on a woollen jacket and cap. He never went out without his cap.

Alice

First, Alice put on a long white chemise made of cotton. It reached to just below her knees. She pulled on a pair of long cotton drawers. The legs of the drawers showed below the chemise. Next, Alice pulled on a pair of black woollen stockings. They came up over her knees. After that she put on a long dress made of blue wool. She needed help to fasten the long row of buttons down the back of her dress.

Over her dress Alice wore a white cotton pinafore. It was a little shorter than the dress. It covered most of her dress except for the sleeves and collar. Alice's boots were the same as Henry's. Before she went out Alice put on a blue straw bonnet with a white ribbon around it. She never went out without her bonnet.

Photocopiable

◆ Dictionary of clothes ◆

✦ Read the words.
✦ Write the words on the dictionary pages.

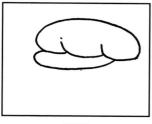

cap

pinafore

dress

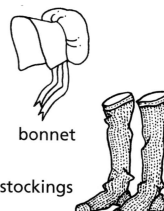

bonnet

stockings

boots

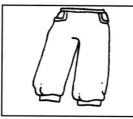

breeches

jacket

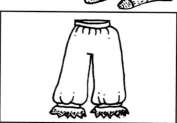

drawers

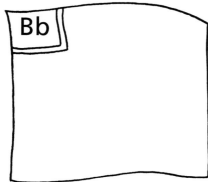

Bb

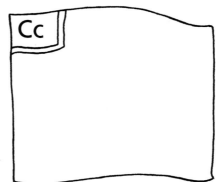

Cc

Dd

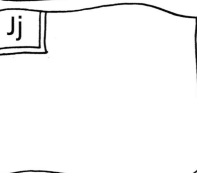

Jj

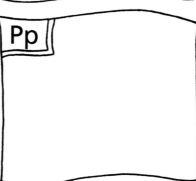

Pp

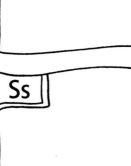

Ss

✦ Draw some of your clothes on the back of this sheet.
✦ Write the words. Circle the first letter.

◆ Dictionary of clothes ◆

✦ Circle the first letter of each word.
✦ Write those letters on the dictionary pages in alphabetical order.
✦ Then write the names of the clothes on the correct pages.

cap   pinafore   dress   bonnet

stockings

boots   breeches   jacket   drawers

Bb

✦ Draw other dictionary pages. On them write the words for other clothes that children used to wear.

◆ Dictionary of clothes ◆

✦ On the dictionary pages write the words for:
- Henry's and Alice's clothes
- the material of the clothes
- the fastenings.

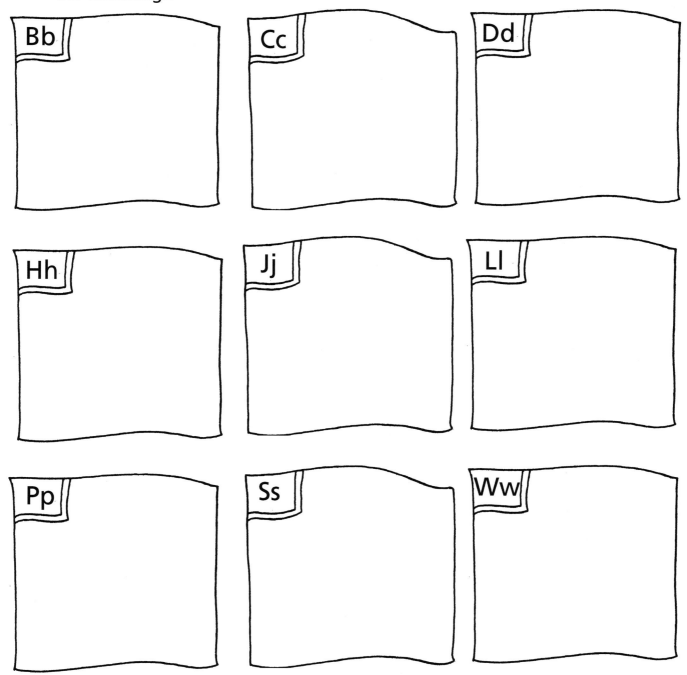

✦ On the back of this sheet, list the clothes you wear.
✦ Then list the materials and the fastenings.

Homes long ago

 Literacy objectives

+ To read instructions. (Y1, T1: T13)
+ To write and draw simple instructions. (Y1, TI: T16)

 History objectives

(Unit 2)
+ To recognise household objects from a long time ago.
+ To describe the characteristics of household objects from a long time ago.
+ To answer questions about household objects from a long time ago.

 Resources

+ Objects used in the laundry in Victorian times: a washboard, a bar of household soap, wooden clothes pegs, a flat-iron and, if possible, a washtub and a mangle, or pictures of them.
+ Photographs and paintings of household items and scenes from Victorian times, for example *Washing Day* by Pierre Edouard Frère (1868) and soap advertisements from the Unilever collection, such as *Besieged* (postcards available from the Lady Lever Gallery and the Port Sunlight Heritage Centre, Port Sunlight, Cheshire).

 Starting point: Whole class

+ Show the children pictures of rooms in a Victorian house. Ask them to name each room (for example, bedroom, kitchen). Which of these rooms do they have in their own homes? Which rooms do they have that are not shown in the Victorian home? Explain that only well-off people had bathrooms and that for many people the only source of water was a cold tap in the kitchen or scullery. Show pictures of backyards with outdoor privies. Write the new vocabulary on the board and explain the meanings of words such as 'privy', 'scullery', 'larder', 'pantry' and 'parlour'.

+ Ask the children to describe the objects they see in the rooms and to name any they can. Which objects are similar to ones they have in their own homes? Help them to identify the objects they can recognise, those which resemble objects in their own homes but are different, and objects they cannot recognise, for example a companion set, range, trivet and washstand.

+ Begin word banks of present-day and old household objects.

+ Show the children items used for laundry in Victorian times (or replicas or pictures of them): a washboard, a bar of household soap, wooden clothes pegs, a flat-iron, a washtub and a mangle. Ask the children to describe the objects and to say how they think they were used. How do they think people heated the flat-iron? Explain that it was heated on a fire. Label and display the objects.

 Using the photocopiable text

+ Photocopy and enlarge the text 'How to wash a shirt' on page 24. Tell the children you are going to read some instructions for washing a shirt, using the household things which people had a long time ago. Before reading, talk about the important features of instructions: a list of the things needed and each step numbered and in the correct order. Ask the children why it is useful to have a list of equipment at the start of a set of instructions. What problems would they have if the instructions were not written in the correct order? Make a separate copy of page 24 and cut out two or more of the stages, cover the numbers and reread the instructions. When you come to a gap, ask the children which instruction belongs in it.

+ Read the list of things needed and invite the children to see if they can find, and point to, the objects in the pictures. Help them to read the names of the unfamiliar objects and to notice critical features of the words: their length, shape and letter combinations.

+ Read the instructions while the children follow them. Point to the picture of each item (or the object itself, if you have it) as you mention it. Invite the children to mime how to use it.

+ Tell the children that they are now going to write their own set of instructions by looking at labelled pictures showing household objects used for making tea a long time ago. Read the labels of the items in the pictures and ensure that the children can read words such as 'pour', 'boiling' and 'fill'.

Homes long ago

 Group activities

Using the differentiated activity sheets

Activity sheet 1: This is for children who need a lot of support in writing instructions. They are required to cut out a set of instructions and put them in the correct order.

Activity sheet 2: This is for children who can read simple consonant-vowel-consonant words. They need to understand the important features of instructions (the list of equipment and the order in which the instructions are written) and should be able to complete sentences with words that make sense.

Activity sheet 3: This is for children who can read and write independently and can write sentences. They need to understand the important features of instructions (the list of equipment and the order in which the instructions are written) and can use this understanding when writing instructions.

 Plenary session

◆ Go over the set of instructions for making a cup of tea. Does everyone agree in which order the steps should be taken?

◆ Now suggest another activity for which instructions need to be written in a specific order, such as boiling an egg or making a piece of buttered toast. Write the instructions on the board, with the children telling you the correct order.

 Follow-up ideas for literacy

◆ Talk about making tea today. Ask the children to list all the things needed: cups or mugs, tea bags, electric kettle and water. They could draw and label a diagram.

◆ Encourage the children to begin (or continue) a word bank of household objects from long ago which we do not use today.

◆ Ask the children to draw and write instructions for making simple things in the classroom – for example, a Plasticine model, or a structure made from blocks. Ask them to give their instructions to a partner to try to follow. The partner could say whether or not the instructions were easy to follow and if the task could be carried out by using them.

 Follow-up ideas for history

◆ Compare the ways in which people wash clothes now and long ago. Ask the children what we use today instead of a washtub, a washboard, and a bar of soap, what people use to remove the water from clothes (instead of a mangle), how clothes pegs and lines are similar and how they are different, and in what other ways people can dry clothes nowadays. Explain that before electricity was invented there were no washing machines, spin dryers or tumble dryers.

◆ Provide catalogues from which the children can cut pictures of electrical items used in the home, such as toasters, microwave ovens, vacuum cleaners and electric lights. Ask them to find out what people used instead before electricity was invented. They could look at artefacts and pictures to find out.

◆ Enlist the children's help in converting a model house or home corner to a house from long ago. What would need to be changed and what could stay the same?

Literacy through history

How to wash a shirt

You need:

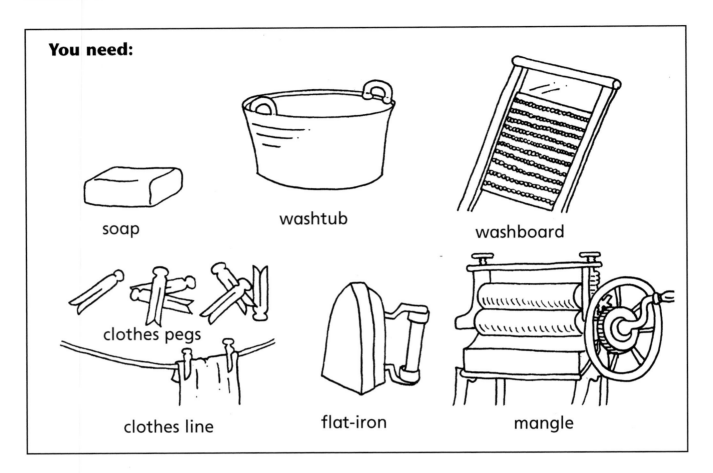

soap

washtub

washboard

clothes pegs

clothes line

flat-iron

mangle

1. Soak the shirt in a tub of hot water.

2. Rub soap on to the shirt.

3. Rub the shirt on the washboard.

4. Rinse the soap off the shirt.

5. Put it through the mangle to squeeze out the water.

6. Peg it on the clothes-line to dry.

7. Heat the flat-iron on the fire.

8. Spread a thick piece of cloth on a table.

9. Spread the dry shirt on the cloth.

10. Smooth it with the hot flat-iron.

Activity 1

◆ How to make tea ◆

✦ Cut out the instructions.
✦ Put them in the correct order. Number the instructions.
✦ Glue them on to a piece of paper.
✦ Write a heading.

You need

kettle

tea

fire

water

teapot

hob

Pour in the boiling water.

Put the kettle on the hob.

Put some tea in the pot.

Fill the kettle with water.

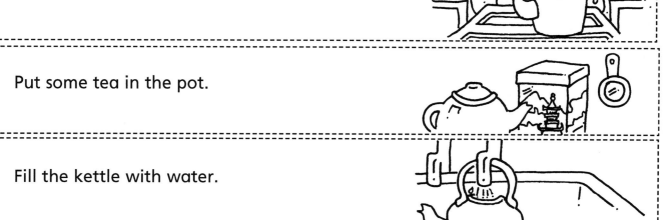

✦ How to make tea ✦

✦ Label the pictures. Use the words on the pad to help you.

fire

hob

kettle

tea

teapot

water

✦ Write instructions for making tea.

Fill the _____
with _____

Put the _____
on the _____

Put some _____
in the _____

Pour in the boiling _____

✦ How to make tea ✦

- ✦ Label the pictures below. Use the words on the pad to help you.
- ✦ Cut out the pictures and put them in order.
- ✦ Write the instructions for making tea. Glue them on to a piece of paper. Number the instructions.
- ✦ Write a heading.

fire
hob
kettle
tea
teapot
water

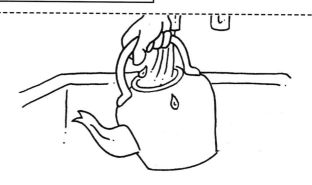

Photocopiable

Seaside holidays in the past

Literacy objectives

✦ To use rhymes as models for their own writing. (Y1, T1: T10)
✦ To use poetry structures as a basis for writing; to invent their own lines. (Y2, T1: T12; Y2, T2: T15)
✦ To identify and discuss patterns of rhyme. (Y2, T2: T9)

History objectives

(Unit 3)
✦ To learn about the features of seaside holidays.
✦ To recall information from their past to answer questions about seaside holidays.
✦ To sequence photographs into a series of three time periods by identifying differences between present and past times.

Resources

✦ Sets of seaside postcards and holiday snapshots (present day and from the times when the children's parents or carers and grandparents were young).

Starting point: Whole class

✦ Ask the children what the word 'holiday' means. On a calendar, show them when the main school holidays are and discuss some of the things that happen during those holidays, such as religious festivals, visits to relatives and family outings. Talk about how holidays are different from other times of the year. Tell the children that the word 'holiday' comes from 'holy day', which means a special day in the Christian Church, such as Easter Sunday or Christmas Day. A long time ago the only holidays people had from school or work were on these holy days. Children from other faith backgrounds might know other words for 'holy days' such as 'mela' or 'purb' (the Hindu and Sikh words, respectively).

✦ Give the children a set of postcards and holiday snapshots from the present day and from the times when their parents or carers and grandparents were young. Challenge them to look at what the people are doing and compare it with what they themselves do when they go the seaside. Ask them to look at what the people are wearing and to notice any clothes which would not be worn on the beach nowadays.

✦ Ask the children, in groups, to put the pictures into three sets: present day; when our parents were young; when our grandparents were young. Agree three things that are similar in the pictures in all three sets and three that are different. Write these on the board.

Using the photocopiable text

✦ Photocopy and enlarge the text 'Sea Song' (page 30) so that all the children can see it. Read the poem while the children follow. Point out the characteristic features of difficult words such as 'murmuring' and 'understand'. Invite the children to read these words with you as you point to the phonemes. Reread the poem, stopping before the last word of line three of each verse to invite the children to supply the missing word.

✦ Mask the words 'land', 'hand' and 'understand' and ask the children to join in as you read the poem again, stopping at the gaps. Challenge the children to remember which words were in the gaps. Point out how the rhyme helps them to remember.

✦ Help the children to memorise the poem by reading the first line and asking them to repeat it, and then reading the first two lines and asking them to repeat them, followed by the first three lines, and so on, building up the whole poem. Once the children have learned the poem, encourage them to recite it to a group of younger children.

✦ Introduce (or revise) the terms 'verse' and 'line'. Tell the children that they are going to write their own verse for the poem 'Sea Song', and that this time they will rhyme with 'sea' instead of 'sand'. For practice, ask them to supply words that rhyme with sea.

Group activities

Using the differentiated activity sheets

Activity sheet 1: This is for children who can match the words and actions of a poem and use picture cues to help them to read and fill in missing words. They are developing an understanding of rhyme and are learning to match words that rhyme.

Activity sheet 2: This is for children who can use pictures as a cue to complete sentences with missing words. They understand what rhyme means and can recognise words

Seaside holidays in the past

that rhyme. They are beginning to use the structure of poems they read as a basis for their own writing.

Activity sheet 3: This is for children who understand what rhyme means; they can recognise words that rhyme and are beginning to use them in their own simple poems based on the structures of those they read.

 Plenary session

✦ Invite the children who completed Activity sheet 1 to take turns to read out a line from their poem. Ask the others to listen and say whether or not it 'sounds right'.

Some of them might be able to explain why it 'sounds right'. Invite the children who completed Activity sheets 2 and 3 to read their poem. Discuss any words they used that were different from those used by the previous group and ask the class if they noticed any rhymes.

✦ Ask the children to read out any rhyming line they have used which makes good sense in their poems, and point out that rhyme *should* make sense. If the class noticed any poems which did not 'sound right', help them to improve the lines by altering the words in order to produce the right rhythm or to create rhymes which make sense.

 Follow-up ideas for literacy

✦ The children could contribute to a class 'rhyming word bank' in which words rhyme with a heading. The word bank could be created in a prepared table on the computer, on a wall display, or in the form of a class book. Encourage the children to continue to add it to it.

ad	ag	am	an	at
bad	bag	dam	gran	cat
glad	drag	jam	man	chat
sad	flag	lamb	ran	flat
	rag	Sam		sat

✦ Share other poems about the seaside. Make up a class collection.

✦ Play word games using rhymes. For example, 'I went shopping and I bought a bat, mat, cat, rat, hat' and so on. If the children have difficulty thinking of words themselves, the game could be played in a circle where each child selects a word from a set written on cards.

 Follow-up ideas for history

✦ Ask someone who grew up locally in the 1950s or earlier to bring in items associated with seaside holidays, for example an old camera, bucket and spade, swimsuit, photographs of a picnic, deckchair, beach ball, airbed and sandals. Ask the children to compare these items with things we use today.

✦ Before the visit, discuss what the visitor could bring in and what he or she could tell the children about a visit to the seaside. Where did his or her family go and how did they travel? What did they take with them and what did they do when they got to the beach? Discuss the facilities available at or near the beach (could they buy ice cream, candy floss, pots of

tea and so on, and how was it different from today?) If they took a picnic, what food and drinks did they take and how did they pack them? Were there donkeys on the beach, ice cream sellers, a Punch and Judy show and so on? If there was a fairground, what rides were there and what did it cost to go on them? What stalls were at the fair?

✦ You could prepare for the visit by collecting other information, perhaps from a railway museum, or the museum of a seaside resort, to supplement what the visitor is going to show and talk about.

Sea Song

Sea-shell, sea-shell,
Murmuring sand,
Murmuring sand.

Sea-shell, sea-shell,
Far-away land,
Far-away land.

Sea-shell, sea-shell,
Sing in my hand,
Sing in my hand.

Sea-shell, sea-shell,
I'll understand
You'll understand.

James Kirkup

©Hopscotch Educational Publishing

✦ Sea Song ✦

✦ Write new lines for each verse of the poem 'Sea Song'.

✦ Fill in the gaps with words from the bottom of the page.

Sea-shell, sea-shell,

Wild and _____,

Wild and _____.

Sea-shell, sea-shell,

Sing to _____,

Sing to _____.

Sea-shell, sea-shell,

What can it _____?

What can it _____?

Sea-shell, sea-shell,

You sing of the _____,

You sing of the _____.

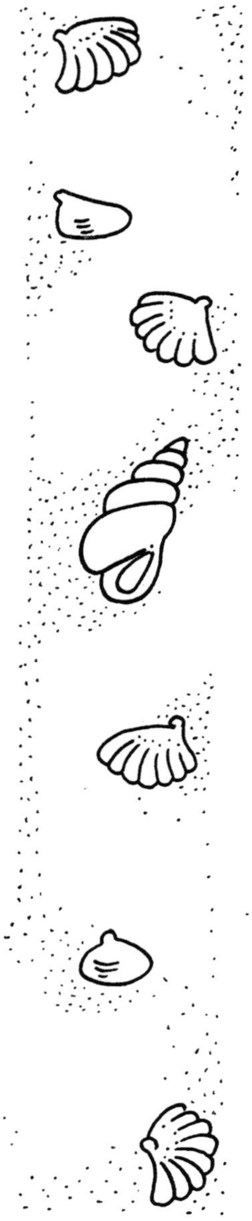

be	me	sea	free

Name _____

◆ S e a   S o n g ◆

✦ Write new lines for each verse of the poem 'Sea Song'.
✦ Fill in the gaps with words that make sense. Use a word bank or dictionary.

Sea-shell, sea-shell,

Wild and _____,

Wild and _____.

Sea-shell, sea-shell,

Sing to _____,

Sing to _____.

Sea-shell, sea-shell,

What can it _____?

What can it _____?

Sea-shell, sea-shell,

You sing of the _____,

You sing of the _____.

✦ Sea Song ✦

✦ Write three new verses for the poem 'Sea Song'.
   One new verse has been written for you.
✦ Use the words in the box to help you.

Useful words
be
free
glee
he
key
knee
me
sea
see
she
tea
tree
we
call
calling
hum
hush
mermaid
sand
shells
smell
sing
singing
song
sound
waves
whisper
whispering

Sea-shell, sea-shell,

Wild and free,

Wild and free.

_____

_____

_____

_____

_____

_____

_____

Florence Nightingale

 ## Literacy objectives

- To understand the purposes of contents pages and begin to locate information by page numbers. (Y1, T2: T21; Y2, T3: T15)
- To identify simple questions and use a text to find answers. (Y1, T3: T19)
- To write their own questions prior to reading. (Y1, T3: T22)

 ## History objectives

(Unit 4)

- To learn about the life of a famous person from the past and why she acted as she did.
- To infer information from a written account of someone's life.
- To locate on a map the site of a historical event.
- To ask questions about the life of Florence Nightingale.

 ## Resources

- A photograph of Florence Nightingale and a photograph of her statue at the Florence Nightingale Museum (available from the Florence Nightingale Museum, 2 Lambeth Palace Road, London SE1 7EW Tel: 0207 620 0374).
- Information books on Florence Nightingale, and other famous people, that have a contents page.
- A map showing the location of the Crimea.

 ## Starting point: Whole class

- Show the children pictures of Florence Nightingale. Ask them if they think she is still alive, lived recently or lived a long time ago. How can they tell? (Talk about the style of her clothing and hair.) Ask the children to describe what they can see in the pictures. Tell them that she was the first British woman to train seriously as a nurse and to take charge of a hospital.

- Explain that Britain joined France and Turkey to fight against Russia in the Crimean War. Show them the location of the Crimea on a map and explain that the Russians wanted to control the lands there. How would people get to Turkey today? Would it take a long time? Say that in Florence Nightingale's time it took 14 days, going by horse-drawn stagecoach and steamship. Show the children the route across France to the port of Marseille, from where a ship could sail to the Black Sea.

 ## Using the photocopiable text

- Photocopy and enlarge the text 'Florence Nightingale' on page 36. Tell the children that they are going to hear about how she became a nurse. Read the recount while the children follow it. Is it fiction or non-fiction? How can they tell? Ask them what facts it tells them about Florence Nightingale. Record these facts in the first column of a chart such as the one below, which can be completed as the discussion progresses.

What we know	What we want to find out	Where we can find out
She was born in 1820	Where was she born?	A video about her life Books about her life

- What else would the children like to know about Florence Nightingale? For example, where she was born, where she lived, what her education was like and what it was like in hospitals in Britain. Help the children to express these ideas in the form of questions. Write them in the second column of the chart. Introduce (or revise) the use of question marks and 'question words' such as 'where', 'when', 'how' and 'why'.

- Ask the children how they could find the answers to their questions. Write their ideas in the third column of the chart. Show them the collection of books (some of which will help them and some which will not), and ask them which ones might be useful. How can they tell? Discuss the titles of the books and other information on their covers (back and front). Revise vocabulary about books: front cover, back cover, illustrations, title page, contents and page headings.

- Look at the contents pages. Talk about what they are for and what information we can get from them. Use one to check that one of the chapters listed starts on the page stated. Agree this list of chapters and page numbers is useful for finding your way round a book.

- Tell the children that they are going to do some work on finding information from books. Make sure they can recognise new words or words with difficult spellings such as 'nurse', 'hospital', 'Crimea', 'weapons', 'ward', 'soldier' and 'medicine'.

Florence Nightingale

 ## Group activities

Using the differentiated activity sheets

Activity sheet 1: This is for children who can read high-frequency words, such as 'what', 'which' and 'did' and are beginning to infer meaning from context. They are developing skills in finding information.

Activity sheet 2: This is for children who can read some high-frequency words and infer meaning from context. They know that a page heading tells the reader what the page is about and are beginning to use a contents page to decide which pages they need.

Activity sheet 3: This is for children who know that a page heading tells the reader what the page is about and who can use a contents page to check page headings to decide on which pages they can find the answers to questions. They are developing skills in writing their own questions prior to reading for information.

 ## Plenary session

✦ Invite the children who completed Activity sheet 1 to share their answers with the class and ask them how they decided which pages would give them the answers to the questions. Display an enlarged copy of Activity sheet 2 and ask the children who completed it to read out their answers, while the others check that they have not omitted any pages which might be useful.

✦ Return to the chart on which you recorded what the children know about Florence Nightingale and what they wanted to find out. Ask the children who completed Activity sheet 3 if they thought of any other questions; write their questions on the chart. Ask them on which pages of the book shown on the activity sheet they can find the answers.

 ### Follow-up ideas for literacy

✦ Provide information books and ask the children to look at the contents pages. Challenge them to decide on which pages they can find the answers to the questions on Activity sheets 1 and 2, or their own questions. Ask them to make a note of the page numbers.

✦ Show the children how to scan a page to decide whether it does, in fact, help them, and to say briefly what the page is about.

✦ The children could use the pages they have located to find the answers to their questions. Ask them to choose some questions to which they can write the answers. The questions and answers could be displayed or stuck into a class book about Florence Nightingale. To reinforce and develop skills in locating information, the children could find the answers to questions posed in other subjects – for example, science and geography.

 ### Follow-up ideas for history

✦ Provide pictures of hospitals and nurses from the present day and from the early nineteenth century. Ask the children to say what they can see in the pictures, and what similarities and differences they notice.

✦ Explain, simply, how the Crimean War began. Show the children pictures of some of the battles and discuss what they can see in the pictures. What do the children know about wars today? Ask them to name some of the weapons they know about. Discuss the similarities and differences between

warfare then and now – for example, there were no bombs, mines or tanks, but the soldiers used rifles and cannon. Tell them how we know what it was like on the battlefields of the Crimea (from pictures by artists who were there, such as William Simpson, reports written for *The Times* newspaper by William Russell and books written by people who were there). This could lead to work on some of these people, including the Jamaican nurse Mary Seacole and Alexis Soyer (the chef from the Reform Club whose work in the Crimea made huge improvements to the diet of soldiers).

Florence Nightingale was born in 1820. Her family was rich and they helped the poor people in the villages near their two homes as much as they could. Florence often visited people who were sick and helped to look after them. She told her parents that she wanted to be a nurse. This did not please them. Rich ladies did not become nurses; it was like being a servant.

So Florence agreed to travel abroad instead with some friends of her parents. She went to Germany, and while she was there she met some people who ran a hospital and trained nurses. She also went to hospitals in France. Nurses there were being trained properly and great care was taken to keep the hospitals clean. In Britain nobody trained nurses: any woman could call herself a nurse and work in a hospital or earn money by looking after sick people in their homes.

When she was thirty Florence went back to Germany. She spent three months training as a nurse. When she came back to England she became Superintendent of Nursing at a small hospital in London.

A man named Sidney Herbert, the Minister of War, knew about Florence's work. He was looking for someone to care for soldiers wounded in battle. They were fighting in the Crimea on the very edge of Europe, near to Russia and Turkey. He asked Florence if she would take charge of some nurses and go to the Crimea.

In 1854, Florence Nightingale set off for the Crimea with 38 nurses. It took them 14 days to get there.

©Hopscotch Educational Publishing

✦ Finding out ✦

✦ Read the children's questions below.
✦ Which pages will help them? Write the number next to the question.

 What did nurses do?

 Where is the Crimea?

 What were hospitals like?

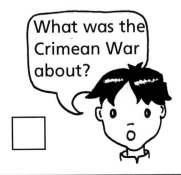 What was the Crimean War about?

 What weapons did the soldiers have?

 What medicines did the nurses have?

Photocopiable

✦ Finding out ✦

✦ Here is the contents page of a book about the Crimean War.

Contents

Florence Nightingale	2	The British Army	14
Nursing	4	A soldier and his weapons	16
The nurse's day	6	Ships	18
Hospitals in Britain	8	The hospital at Scutari	20
The Crimean War	10	Medicines	22
A map of the Crimea	12	Index	24

✦ Which pages will help these children answer their questions?
Write the page numbers in the boxes.

What did nurses do?

Where is the Crimea?

What were hospitals like?

What was the Crimean war about?

What weapons did the soldiers have?

What medicines did the nurses have?

Activity 3

◆ Finding out ◆

◆ Write three questions about Florence Nightingale.

Remember the question marks.

_____ ☐

_____ ☐

_____ ☐

◆ Write a question about the Crimean War.

_____ ☐

◆ Write a question about hospitals.

_____ ☐

◆ Here is the contents page of a book about the Crimean War. Next to your questions, write the numbers of the pages that might help you.

Contents

Florence Nightingale	2	The British Army	14
Nursing	4	A soldier and his weapons	16
The nurse's day	6	Ships	18
Hospitals in Britain	8	The hospital at Scutari	20
The Crimean War	10	Medicines	22
A map of the Crimea	12	Index	24

©Hopscotch Educational Publishing

George Stephenson

Literacy objectives

- To scan a text to find specific sections. (Y2, T3: T16)
- To answer questions posed about a specific text.

History objectives

(Unit 4)
- To learn about some of the improvements made by George Stephenson.
- To learn to infer information about a person's life from a written source.
- To learn why George Stephenson is remembered today.

Resources

- Information books about George Stephenson.
- Pictures of colliery wagonways, stationary steam engines, steam locomotives and the wagons they pulled.

Starting point: Whole class

- Tell the children they are going to learn about a man named George Stephenson who developed the first railway for people to travel on. Show the children pictures of colliery wagonways. Say that these were the first trains and that they were pulled along wooden tracks by horses or even by people. Tell them that wagonways were used even in ancient times. Encourage them to suggest why the wagonways were built. Ask why they think the horses only pulled the wagons uphill and, sometimes, on level ground. What problem had to be solved when the wagons were allowed to roll downhill? You could demonstrate, using models.

- If possible, show the children a working model of a steam engine (available from educational suppliers). Explain how it works, pointing out the turbine driven by the power of the steam and how the movement of the turbine can be used to move other things. Show them a picture of a stationary steam engine and point out the cables that were attached to the wagons to pull them along the tracks.

- Tell the children that a number of engineers in collieries and other mines were trying to build steam engines on wheels which would go along the tracks. Show them pictures of the early locomotives built by Richard

Trevithick and William Hedley. Tell them about the problems caused by the very heavy weight of the locomotives (breaking wheels and tracks) and explain why George Stephenson's locomotives were important. (He found a way to make stronger wheels and tracks.)

Using the photocopiable text

- Photocopy the text 'George Stephenson' (page 42) and give the children copies. Tell them that the text is about the first railways and engines and about a famous railway engineer named George Stephenson. Read the recount while the children follow it. Ask them if it is a fiction or non-fiction text, and how they can tell.

- Model how to use the text to find the answers to questions. For example, 'How did people travel around the country before railways were built?' Point out the key word ('travel') and show the children how to scan the text to find it. It may be helpful to 'think aloud' about what you are doing. Highlight the word 'travel' and ask the children what the text tells them. Model how to answer other questions: write the question on the board, show the children how to scan the text, ask them to answer the question and then write their answer on the board. Ask the others if the answer can be improved, and how.

- Tell the children that some of them are going to use this text about George Stephenson to help them to answer questions about him and that others will use a different text. Encourage them to look for key words in the questions and underline those words in the text.

Group activities

Using the differentiated activity sheets

Activity sheet 1: This is for children who are learning how to scan a text to identify key words that will help them to locate information and are developing skills in using the information they find to answer a simple question. They are not yet ready to write whole sentences about the text but can complete partially-written sentences.

George Stephenson

Activity sheet 2: This is for children who are developing skills in scanning a text to identify key words that will help them to locate information and can use the information they find to answer a simple question. They are developing skills in writing the answer to a question in complete sentences.

Activity sheet 3: This is for children who are developing skills in deciding what information is needed in order to answer more difficult questions. They can scan a text to identify key words that will help them to locate information and can write a sentence to answer the question.

 Plenary session

+ Invite the children who completed Activity sheets 1 and 2 to share their answers with the class and ask them to point out the key words in the text that they underlined to answer the questions. Did the others underline the same words? Ask them to explain their choices. Invite them to read out their answers. The others should check that the sentence really does answer the question. Invite the children who completed Activity sheet 3 to take turns to read out questions and identify the key words they underlined. What information helped them to answer the question? Ask them to explain their answers.

 Follow-up ideas for literacy

+ Provide information books about George Stephenson and the development of railways and show the children how to use the index to find the pages that will help them to answer a question.

+ Show the children how to make notes from different books, using abbreviations. They could make a word bank of abbreviations for notes.

Short ways to write		
Days	**Months**	**Long words**
Mon (Monday)	Jan (January)	hosp (hospital)
Tues (Tuesday)	Feb (February)	rway (railway)
Wed (Wednesday)	Mar (March)	loc (locomotive)

 Follow-up ideas for history

+ Give each group a set of six cards on which are written statements about the things George Stephenson did to help railways to develop. For example:
'He invented a way to make steel stronger.'
'With his son, he built a locomotive which beat all the others at the Rainhill Trials.'
'He built the railway at Hetton Colliery.'
'He designed railway bridges.'
'He found ways of taking railways across difficult land to save going round it.'
'He built the world's first passenger railway.'
Ask the children to put the statements in order of importance, and invite them to talk about their choices.

+ Ask the children to write non-chronological accounts of the differences that George Stephenson made to travel for people and the transport of goods. Provide books about, and pictures of, transport before and after the development of railways.

+ Link this work with work on seaside holidays in the past: show the children copies of railway posters; first-, second- and third-class tickets (and carriages); advertisements for seaside outings and holidays. You could also show them paintings of people travelling by train from the time.

George Stephenson

George Stephenson was born in 1781 in Wylam, a coal-mining village near Newcastle. His father worked in the pit there.

To travel in those days people had to walk, ride a horse or go in a cart (or, if they could afford it, a stage-coach). Rich people had their own carriages pulled by horses. The roads were tracks of hard earth which turned to mud when it rained. Wheels and horses' hooves made holes in the mud. When the mud dried, the roads were bumpy and dusty.

Ships carried goods along rivers and canals and from port to port around the coast of Britain. Horses walked along the banks of canals to pull the canal boats. The power of steam had been discovered and steamships were being built. These ships had boilers heated by coal fires.

Railways had been used for a long time in mines to pull heavy wagons. Horses, and even people, pulled the wagons along the tracks. Now steam engines were being built. They did not move, but pulled the trucks uphill using ropes; the trucks were left to roll downhill and had brakes to slow them down.

George Stephenson heard that Richard Trevithick had built a steam locomotive in Cornwall and that William Hedley had built one named 'Puffing Billy' at a colliery near Newcastle.

A locomotive is a steam engine on wheels running along railway lines. The locomotives had problems: they were so heavy that they broke the tracks and even their own wheels. George found a way to make steel stronger. He built a railway at Hetton Colliery. His tracks and wheels were much stronger.

George Stephenson and his son Robert also built a railway between the coalfields near Darlington and the port of Stockton-on-Tees. People and companies paid to run their own carriages and wagons on the railway, pulled by horses.

After that, the Stephensons built the Liverpool to Manchester Railway. It had steam locomotives pulling goods wagons and passenger coaches. To find the best locomotive, the railway company held a competition called the Rainhill Trials. The Stephensons' locomotive, 'Rocket', won.

Photocopiable

◆ Answering questions ◆

✦ Read this information about George Stephenson.

George Stephenson left school when he was twelve years old. He went to work with his father at a colliery. Many machines were used in collieries. There was no electricity then. Steam was used for power.

George was very good at fixing machinery. When he was fourteen he was made assistant fireman.

The firemen looked after the steam engine. This engine drove the machines. George found clever ways to change the machines and soon he was put in charge of the steam engine. George wanted to learn more about machines but he could not read very well or do mathematics. So he paid a teacher to give him lessons in the evenings.

✦ Now read these questions. Fill in the gaps in the answers.

 How old was George when he left school?

George Stephenson was _____ when he left school.

 Where was his first job?

His first job was at _____

 What were the men who looked after the steam engine called?

The men who looked after the steam engine were called _____

 There was something George did very well. What was it?

The thing George did very well was

_____

 What kind of engine did George look after?

He looked after a _____

_____

 How did George Stephenson learn to read?

He paid a _____

◆ Answering questions ◆

✦ Read this information about George Stephenson.

George Stephenson left school when he was twelve years old. He went to work with his father at a colliery. Many machines were used in collieries. There was no electricity then. Steam was used for power.

George was very good at fixing machinery. When he was fourteen he was made assistant fireman. The firemen looked after the steam engine. This engine drove the machines. George found clever ways to change the machines and soon he was put in charge of the steam engine.

George wanted to learn more about machines but he could not read very well or do mathematics. So he paid a teacher to give him lessons in the evenings.

✦ Now read these questions then write the answers.

 Where was George Stephenson's first job?

_____

_____

 What were the men who looked after the steam engine called?

_____

_____

 There was something George did very well. What was it?

_____

_____

 How did George Stephenson learn to read?

_____

_____

◆ Answering questions ◆

◆ Read the passage about George Stephenson again to help you to answer the questions below.

◆ Write your answers in sentences.

 Why were heavy loads not carried by road?

_____

_____

_____

 What is the difference between a steam locomotive and a steam engine?

_____

_____

_____

 What problem did Richard Trevithick and William Hedley have with their locomotives?

_____

_____

_____

 What did George Stephenson do to solve this problem?

_____

_____

_____

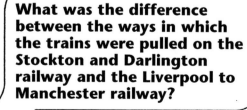 **What was the difference between the ways in which the trains were pulled on the Stockton and Darlington railway and the Liverpool to Manchester railway?**

_____

_____

_____

Chapter 8

The Great Fire of London

 ## Literacy objectives

◆ To understand the difference between fact and fiction. (Y2, T3: T13)
◆ To make simple notes from non-fiction texts. (Y2, T3: T19)

 ## History objectives

(Unit 5)
◆ To learn about where the Great Fire of London broke out and how and when it happened; comparing London then with now.
◆ To place the Great Fire of London on a timeline.

 ## Resources

◆ Pictures of central London today, including the area around Monument underground station and the Monument itself, St Paul's Cathedral and a modern building (such as the BT Tower).
◆ Pictures of ordinary people from the mid-seventeenth century and of Charles II.
◆ A map of the United Kingdom.

 ## Starting point: Whole class

◆ Show the children a picture of central London that features a well-known site, and ask them if they know which city it is and which country it is in. On a map of the UK, point out London and your school's locality.

◆ Tell the children that London is a very old city. Show them pictures of today's and older buildings, such as the British Telecom Tower, Hampton Court Palace and St Paul's Cathedral. How can they tell the difference between old and modern buildings?

◆ Show the children pictures of people who lived in the mid-seventeenth century and ask them to describe what they see. Tell them that the people lived a long time ago – a long time before their great-grandparents – when Charles II was king. Explain that when these people were alive there was a great fire in London, which burned down most of the city. Introduce them to the term 'The Stuarts' and help them to place the period on a time-line.

 ## Using the photocopiable text

◆ Photocopy the text 'The Monument' (page 48) and give the children copies or use it on an OHP. Explain that the text is about a part of London that was rebuilt after the fire and about a famous monument built there. Ask them if the text is fiction or non-fiction, and how they can tell. (Point out that it is about a real place and real events which can be checked.) Discuss the features of non-fiction texts that are not usually found in fiction: a map, a caption and sub-headings. Read the sub-headings and ask the children what they think each section of the report will tell them.

◆ Read the report while the children follow it. Discuss the meaning of the term 'fact'. Give some examples. Ask them to notice any facts that it gives. Invite suggestions as to how these facts could be checked.

◆ Ask the children if there are any words they do not understand. Reread these words and write them on the board. Explain what they mean. Begin a 'Great Fire of London' word bank, to which the children can add as they come across words in their reading.

◆ Talk to the children about making notes. Demonstrate to them how we can extract pieces of information and make notes about them. Using the second paragraph of the text, underline key words such as '60 metres high', 'round column', 'stone', 'urn' and 'copper'. Write these words on the board, explaining that notes are not usually sentences but can be words and short phrases that tell us the most important things. Explain how to use headings to locate things, such as 'In which section would we find out why the Monument was built?'

◆ Tell the children that now they are going to make notes about the Monument to help them to remember the important facts.

Group activities

Using the differentiated activity sheets

Activity sheet 1: This is for children who are beginning to use headings to find their way around a text. They are learning to make notes with the support of prepared headings and phrases with gaps to fill in. They understand the meaning of 'fact' and can make statements about facts.

The Great Fire of London

Activity sheet 2: This is for children who can use headings to find their way around a text. They understand the meaning of 'fact' and can identify facts in the text. They are developing skills in making notes with the support of prepared headings and phrases with gaps to fill in.

Activity sheet 3: This is for children who have a secure understanding of the meaning of the term 'fact' and can use sub-headings and captions to help them to identify facts in a text. They can make notes about a text with the help of a structure that provides headings for their notes, and are beginning to make their own headings for their notes.

 Plenary session

✦ Invite the children who completed Activity sheets 1 an 2 to read out their completed 'postcards' and 'fact files'. Ask them what facts they have learned about the Monument and the Great Fire of London. Ask the children who completed Activity sheets 3 to add any other facts they have learned. Ask them to explain what helped them to talk about the Monument and the Great Fire of London without looking at the text. Reinforce their understanding of the purpose of notes: to help them to remember the important things they have read.

 Follow-up ideas for literacy

✦ Ask the children to use their notes to write their own report about the Monument and the Great Fire of London. Before they begin, encourage them to make a sketch of the Monument from a photograph or picture postcard and label the parts of it about which they have learned. They should write a caption for their picture. Ask them to re-read the headings on their notes. How can the headings help them to organise their writing?

✦ Discuss the questions raised by the text: for example, how did the fire begin in the bakery, how did it spread to the buildings next door, and across the whole city? The children could use information

books, CD-Roms and videos to find out about the Great Fire of London and about Samuel Pepys.

✦ Discuss the effects of using different words when writing about an event. For example, the verb 'raged' is used in the text. Ask the children to describe how this is different from 'burned'. They could think of other words for 'burn' (using a thesaurus), for example 'glow', 'smoulder' and 'singe', and say what sort of fire each one makes them imagine. Similarly, they could look through the text for words that mean 'go' or 'goes' and explain how each one is different. How many different words for 'go' can they think of?

 Follow-up ideas for history

✦ Give the children a series of cards on which there is a description of an event during the Great Fire of London. Ask them to put the cards in order. Show them copies of Samuel Pepys' Diary and the *London Gazette* and tell them that we know about the fire from written sources such as these.

✦ In connection with their work in literacy, the children could list the factors which made the fire spread very easily. Help them to find out about fire-fighting procedures then and now and what lessons were learned from the Great Fire of London about the safety of buildings and about being prepared for fire. They could make a list of fire safety and fire-fighting instructions for a city of the time.

Useful websites include:
www.gloscc.gov.uk/pubserv/gcc/fire/history/grtfire.htm
www.jmccall.demon.co.uk/history
www.thehistorynet.com/BritishHeritage/articles/1995_text.htm
www.britainexpress.com/History/great_fire.htm
The London Fire Brigade Museum also has information: Winchester House, 94A Southwark Bridge Road, London SE1 0UG.

✦ Tell the children about the work of Sir Christopher Wren. Show them postcards of some of the buildings that he and others designed to replace those burned in the Great Fire of London, such as St Paul's Cathedral and many other churches.

The Monument

The site

As soon as you come out of Monument Underground station in London you can tell how it got its name. A tall column reaches into the sky – the Monument.

The outside of the Monument

The Monument is more than 60 metres high – much taller than any of the buildings around it. It is a round column, made from stone, standing on a square base. At the top of it is a bright urn (a kind of vase) made from copper.

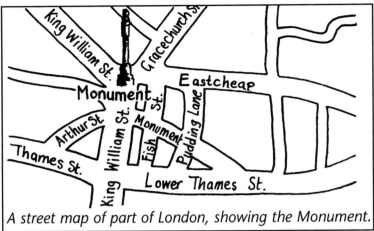

A street map of part of London, showing the Monument.

The Monument, designed by Sir Christopher Wren and Robert Hooke and built in 1671.

Inside the Monument

There is a door in the base of the Monument and you can go inside. A notice says that it is open every day from ten o'clock in the morning until six o'clock in the evening. To go in costs £1.50 for an adult and 50 pence for a child under 16. All that is inside is a spiral staircase leading right up to the top – 311 steps. You are given a certificate for getting to the top.

Why it was built

There is some writing on the base, in Latin. It says that the height of the Monument is also the distance from where it stands to the place where the Great Fire of London began – just over 60 metres. The fire began on 2 September 1666. It broke out at night in a bakery in Pudding Lane and raged through the city. The wooden buildings with their thatched roofs burned easily. The only way to stop the fire was to blow up some houses with gunpowder. That made a space so that there was nothing for the fire to burn and, after five days, the fire went out.

©Hopscotch Educational Publishing

◆ N o t e s ◆

✦ Read the facts about the Monument.
✦ Complete the postcard.

The Monument was built to mark the Great Fire of London. It is near Monument Underground station in London. It was built in 1671 near the place where the fire began. The Monument is more than 60 metres high and 311 steps lead up to the top. You can go inside. It costs £1.50 for an adult and 50 pence for a child under 16 to go in.

POSTCARD

The Monument

City _____ **Date built** _____

Site Near _____ Underground station

Height _____ metres   **Number of steps** _____

Why it was built   To mark the _____

_____

Cost to go inside   Adult _____

Child _____

✦ Write another fact about the Monument.

_____

_____

◆ N o t e s ◆

✦ Complete the fact-file about the Monument.

The Monument

Place
City _____
Site Near to _____ Underground station

Why it was built
To mark the

_____

in the year _____ .

Facts about the Monument
Date built _____
Number of steps _____
Height _____ metres
Why is it that height?   The _____ of London began
_____ metres from there.

Designers
_____ and

_____

Facts about the Great Fire of London

Began in a _____ in _____ Lane.

Began on _____

Burned for _____ days.

◆ Notes ◆

✦ Complete the fact-file about the Monument.
✦ Write other headings. Write information under these headings.

The Monument

City	
Site	
Why it was built	**Date built**
Height	**Number of steps**
Why is it that height?	
Designers	

Remembrance Day

 ## Literacy objectives

- To understand that dictionaries give definitions and explanations. (Y2, T2: T17)
- To make dictionaries and glossaries giving definitions. (Y2, T2: T20)
- To learn new words from reading linked to particular topics. (Y2, T2: W10)

 ## History objectives

(Unit 17)

- To learn that symbols may represent commemorative events and why particular symbols are associated with commemorations.
- To learn that commemorations are linked to specific events in the past that really happened.
- To learn when World War I and Armistice Day occurred.
- To learn how some historic events are commemorated every year.

 ## Resources

- A picture of the Remembrance Day memorial service at the Cenotaph in London.
- Poppies in the different arrangements produced for the annual Royal British Legion Poppy Appeal.

 ## Starting point: Whole class

- Show the children a photograph of the Remembrance Day memorial service at the Cenotaph in London. What does the word 'cenotaph' mean? Together look it up in a dictionary. (You may need to use an adult dictionary.) Write the word and its definition on the board. Draw out the importance of the occasion. Notice the people in uniform, such as members of the armed forces, including those wounded in action.

- Tell the children that Remembrance Day services are held every year in memory of soldiers killed or injured in wars. Talk about any other events about which the children know or in which they take part each year. Introduce the term 'anniversary'. Again write the word and its definition on the board. Ask them if the events are sad or happy.

- Do the children know the date of Remembrance Day and why that date was chosen?

- Show them examples of the poppies that are sold each year during the Poppy Appeal. Why are the poppies sold? Explain that the poppy became a symbol of remembrance of the soldiers who died in World War I, later of those killed in World War II, and now of soldiers killed in other wars. Do the children know why the poppy are sold? Tell them that they can find the answer in the text they are going to read.

- Talk about the meanings of the words 'symbol', 'memorial' and 'remembrance'. Model again how to look words up in a dictionary, pointing out the definitions and explaining the term 'definition'. Show the children how to find the correct part of the dictionary by asking questions such as 'If the word begins with "m", will it be near the front, back or middle of the dictionary?' Having found the appropriate section of the dictionary, ask questions such as 'Is it before or after "p"?', 'Which way shall I turn the pages?' and 'This page begins with "make", so might the word be on this page?' Some children might need an alphabet strip.

 ## Using the photocopiable text

- Photocopy and enlarge the text 'Remembrance Day' (page 54). Tell the children they are going to hear about a Remembrance Day service at the cenotaph in Liverpool. Remind them of the questions that arose earlier and ask them if they think the passage might help them to answer the questions. Look at the picture and caption to find out at which cenotaph this Remembrance Day service took place.

- Read the passage while the children follow it. Stop at the new words ('remembrance', 'cenotaph', 'World War I' and 'memorial'). Challenge the children to read the words. Remind them of their meanings.

- After reading the passage, ask the children if it helps them to answer any of their questions, and what answers they have found.

- Tell them that now they will be using dictionaries and the words on the board to help them complete an activity sheet.

Remembrance Day

 ## Group activities

Using the differentiated activity sheets

Activity sheet 1: This is for children who are beginning to use dictionaries to check the meanings of words as well as their spellings. They are developing skills in reading definitions and matching them to words. They know the alphabet and are developing skills in ordering words alphabetically by the first letter. They need help in ordering words by the first and second letters.

Activity sheet 2: This is for children who are developing skills in using dictionaries to check definitions as well as spellings. They are developing skills in finding words in texts with given definitions. They know the alphabet and can order words alphabetically by the first letter and are developing an understanding of alphabetical order by second letter also.

Activity sheet 3: This is for children who can use dictionaries to check definitions as well as spellings. They understand what a definition is and can find words with given definitions. They know the alphabet and can order words alphabetically by the first and second letters. They are developing skills in writing definitions.

Plenary session

✦ Talk to the children about any local war memorials. Do they know where they are? Can anyone describe one of them? Does it have names on it or dates? Is there a picture or sculpture? Together draw a picture on the board of what everyone thinks it looks like. Label where the different parts are. If possible, visit a memorial with the children. Alternatively, take photos to show them.

 ## Follow up-ideas for literacy

✦ Ask the children to make a chart of questions and answers. For example, 'When was World War I?', 'When was World War II?', 'What happened when the Armistice was signed?' and 'Who signed it?'.

✦ Model how to check if an information text will help to answer the questions (looking at the pictures and reading the front and back covers, contents page, captions, headings and sub-headings). Show the children how to make a note of useful texts: making a note of the title and author, any useful headings, sub-headings and captions and whether the text is too difficult, too simple or just right. The children could share their notes during a plenary session.

✦ Each day a word connected with a topic about which the children are learning could be displayed, and the children challenged to find its meaning. Their definitions could be displayed, discussed and refined.

Follow-up ideas for history

✦ If possible, arrange to visit a war memorial in the locality. The children could sketch and take photographs of it and make notes about what they see. Discuss the dates and explain anything that seems odd: for example, the dates on some cenotaphs are '1914–1919', rather than the expected '1914–1918' (the year of the ceasefire and Armistice). This is because the first Peace Parade in Britain to celebrate the Armistice was not held until July 1919, after peace settlements were signed with Germany. Also, although some memorials and cenotaphs were built to commemorate soldiers killed in World War I, the dates '1939–1945' were added to them to include those killed in World War II.

✦ Tell the children the story of how the poppy became the symbol of remembrance. A secretary named Moina Michael read John McCrae's poem about the poppies growing where the soldiers were buried on the battlefields in World War I. She grew some poppies which she sold to her friends to raise money to help wounded ex-service people and their families (and the families of those who had been killed). Others began to do the same and, eventually, the British Legion and similar organisations in other countries involved in World War I were formed to help those people.

Remembrance Day

A clock struck eleven. The people around the cenotaph stood still and silent. Most of them wore sombre colours – black, grey or navy blue – and every one of them wore a bright red poppy. Some had their heads bowed; some looked at the poppy wreaths on the steps.

Katy did not move as she held her grandfather's hand. She looked at the scene on the great bronze panel on the side of the cenotaph. It looked just like the scene around her except that it happened a long time ago. She read the words carved in the stone above it:

TO THE MEN OF LIVERPOOL WHO FELL IN THE GREAT WAR.

On the back of the cenotaph was an engraving of soldiers marching with rifles over their shoulders.

Then someone coughed, the people in uniform moved away from the steps, and the minute-long silence was over. Katy asked her grandfather what he had been thinking about. 'My grandfather,' he said. 'He was killed in World War I, before I was born.'

'Is he buried in the cenotaph?' asked Katy.

'No,' he said, 'Nobody is buried in it. "Cenotaph" means "empty tomb". It's a memorial to all the soldiers who died. We remember them on the eleventh hour of the eleventh day of the eleventh month because that was when the Armistice was signed in 1918. It ended World War I.'

'Why do we have the poppies?'

'Because poppies grew wild on the battlefields in Flanders, where so many soldiers were killed and buried,' he said. 'A poem by an army doctor named John McCrae made the poppies famous. I can't remember all of it, but it begins,

In Flanders fields the poppies blow
Between the crosses, row on row...'

©Hopscotch Educational Publishing

◆ Definitions ◆

◆ Cut out the words and definitions.
◆ Match each word to a definition.
◆ Put them in alphabetical order of the words.

Words

cenotaph	tomb	wreath
poppy	war	silent	memorial

Definitions

Something made or built in memory of a person, a group of people or an event.

A band of flowers and leaves fastened together.

A fight, using weapons, between countries or large groups of people.

With no sound.

A large stone box above the ground where a dead person is buried.

A plant with bright flowers.

An empty tomb built to help us remember soldiers killed in battle.

Photocopiable

◆ Definitions ◆

◆ Find the words in the class text that go with the definitions below.
◆ Write the words in the boxes.
◆ Cut out the words and definitions.
◆ Put them in alphabetical order.

Words	Definitions
m_____	Something made or built in memory of a person, a group of people or an event.
w_____	A band of flowers and leaves fastened together.
w_____	A fight, using weapons, between countries or large groups of people.
s_____	With no sound.
t_____	A large stone box above the ground where a dead person is buried.
p_____	A plant with bright flowers.
c_____	An empty tomb built to help us remember soldiers killed in battle.

◆ Definitions ◆

◆ Write a definition for each word.
◆ Cut out the words and definitions.
◆ Put them in alphabetical order.

Words	Definitions
cenotaph	
tomb	
wreath	
poppy	
war	
silent	
memorial	

Chapter 10

The Gunpowder Plot

 Literacy objectives

✦ To understand time and sequential relationships in stories. (Y2, T1: T4)
✦ To use simple organisational devices, for example arrows and boxes. (Y2, T1: S1)
✦ To produce simple flow charts to show the sequence of events in a story. (Y2, T2: T21)
✦ To write non-fiction texts. (Y2, T3: T20)

 History objectives

(Unit 5)
✦ To learn to sequence events correctly.
✦ To learn why an historical event happened.
(Unit 17)
✦ To learn how some historic events are commemorated by celebrations.

 Resources

✦ Pictures of bonfires and fireworks.
✦ A picture of a 'guy' (or a real 'guy').

 Starting point: Whole class

✦ Show the children pictures of bonfires and fireworks and ask them what is happening. Why have the people lit a fire and set off fireworks? Encourage the children to talk about bonfires and fireworks they have experienced. These might be connected with other events as well as Guy Fawkes Night, for example religious festivals and the New Year. Encourage them to talk about events they celebrate every year on the same day and what they do during the celebrations.

✦ Show the children the 'guy' or a picture of one and ask them if they have ever seen one. What do people do with it and when? Do they know why it is called a 'guy'? What do they know about Guy Fawkes Night? Talk about the date on which it is celebrated and what people do as well as setting off fireworks and lighting bonfires. For example, they might eat traditional foods such as roast chestnuts.

✦ Do the children know who Guy Fawkes was? Discuss why there should be celebrations connected with a plot to kill the king and members of the government. Point out that the king was unharmed and the plotters were captured.

✦ Help the children to place the Gunpowder Plot on a timeline along with other events and historical periods about which they have learned.

 Using the photocopiable text

✦ Photocopy the text 'The Gunpowder Plot' on page 60 and give the children copies. Tell them they are going to read the story of the Gunpowder Plot – a true story about a real event. Read the text while they follow it.

✦ Ask the children what the first paragraph is about. Help them to summarise it in a few words, for example 'James, the new king of England'. Write the summary on the board. Read the second paragraph again. Ask the children what that is about. Help them to summarise it. Continue in this way to the end of the text.

✦ Remove the text so that the children cannot see it, and ask them what happened first in it. Encourage them to use the summary to help them to answer. Continue in the same way for each paragraph. Write the children's answers on a flow chart. Point out that they could use the flow chart to help them to retell the story.

✦ Tell the children that they are going to do some work on putting the events of the Gunpowder Plot in the correct order on a flow chart and on retelling the story in their own words. Remind them that they will need to reread the story to check what happened.

 Group activities

Using the differentiated activity sheets

Activity sheet 1: This is for children who are beginning to understand the idea of the time sequence of a story. They are developing skills in putting the events of a story in the correct order with the help of pictures and are learning how to use a flow chart.

Activity sheet 2: This is for children who understand the idea of the time sequence of a story. They can put the events of a story in the correct order with the help of pictures, and understand how to use a flow chart. They are developing skills in making notes.

The Gunpowder Plot

Activity sheet 3: This is for children who have a secure understanding of the idea of the time sequence of a story. They can put the events of a story in the correct order and understand how to use a flow chart. They are developing skills in making notes and in using their notes to rewrite a story.

 Plenary session

✦ Invite the children who completed Activity sheets 1 and 2 to read out the sentences they wrote in the order in which they matched the pictures. Ask the others to check if the pictures are in the correct order and to listen to see if the story makes sense. Help them to check it against the text on page 60. Ask those who completed Activity sheet 3 to read out the notes in the order in which they have arranged them. Invite them to share the sentences which they wrote from their notes.

 Follow-up ideas for literacy

✦ The children could skim-read books to find out what they are about, and say if they will help them to find out more about the Gunpowder Plot. They could scan and evaluate the books, giving them a symbol '+', '=' or '–' to indicate how useful they are for this purpose. Encourage them to record their ideas:

Title	How good it is: + (good); = (fairly good); – (not good)
The Gunpowder Plot	+

✦ Help the children to write a class book about the Gunpowder Plot, planning the headings and sub-headings and pictures and captions they will include. Help them to plan the contents page before they begin, and to number the pages. Different groups could work on different pages, ensuring that the page headings match the headings on the contents page.

✦ Help the children to decide what should be in the index. As a piece of shared writing, they could contribute to the list, arrange it in alphabetical order and then check on which pages the entries appear.

 Follow-up ideas for history

✦ Show the children portraits of Guy Fawkes and the other Gunpowder Plotters. Ask them to describe the pictures and say what they can tell about the people from the pictures. They should notice the style of their clothing, and that they show that the people lived a long time ago.

✦ Read the story of Guy Fawkes' life before the Gunpowder Plot. (See page 64.) Ask the children what they think made him want to become involved in the plot.

✦ The children could sequence the events of Guy Fawkes' life or make a timeline of his life, showing the important events.

✦ Help the children to find out about the life of James VI of Scotland and how he became James I of England through being the son of Mary Queen of Scots.

The Gunpowder Plot

In 1603 Queen Elizabeth died and England had a new monarch. He was James VI of Scotland and he became James I of England, too. James was a Protestant and he decided that everyone in England should become Protestant. That upset many people.

A group of Roman Catholic men met at an inn in London in 1604 to work out a plot to kill the king. They would blow up the House of Lords when the king was there. They took an oath to keep their plans secret. One of the men was Guy Fawkes.

The first five gunpowder plotters at their meeting.

The plotters took lodgings in a house with a storeroom underneath the House of Lords and they began to store barrels of gunpowder there.

The plan was for the other plotters to leave London and for Guy Fawkes to light the fuse on 5 November, the day Parliament opened. He would escape by boat across the River Thames.

At the end of October Lord Mounteagle had a letter telling him about the plot so that he could stay away from Parliament and keep safe. Lord Mounteagle told the other lords.

The lords told the king, and on 4 November, the day before the opening of Parliament, they searched the cellars. They found Guy Fawkes with the gunpowder. He said his name was John Johnson.

Guy Fawkes being caught with the gunpowder.

The king's soldiers took Guy Fawkes to the Tower of London. They tortured him until he told them his real name. He would not say anything else. The longer he kept silent the longer the others would have to get away. By the 7 November he had been tortured so much that he gave the names of some of the other plotters.

A search was set up. They were all caught and put to death. Guy Fawkes was the last to be hanged, on 31 January 1606.

Guy Fawkes being tortured.

✦ A flow chart ✦

✦ Complete the sentences under the pictures.
✦ Put the pictures in order. Glue them on to a piece of paper.
✦ Join the pictures with arrows to make a flow chart.
✦ Draw the last picture. Write a sentence to go with it.

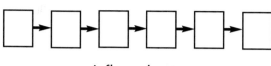

A flow chart

Lord Mounteagle had a _____
_____

The soldiers found _____
_____

A group of men met at _____
_____

The plotters stored _____
_____

Guy Fawkes was _____
_____

Photocopiable

Name _____

◆ A flow chart ◆

✦ Write a sentence under each picture.
✦ Put the pictures in order. Glue them on to a piece of paper.
✦ Join the pictures with arrows to make a flow chart.
✦ Draw the last picture. Write a sentence to go with it.

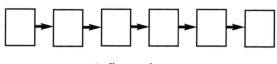

A flow chart

Lord Mounteagle

Name _____

◆ A flow chart ◆

✦ Cut out the notes below and put them in order to tell the story of the Gunpowder Plot. Glue them on to a piece of paper. Join the notes with arrows to make a flow chart.

✦ Write notes for the last part of the flow chart.

✦ Use the notes to rewrite the story of the Gunpowder Plot.

Letter to Lord Mounteagle tells him about the Plot. He tells other Lords.	Cellars of House of Lords searched on 4 Nov. Guy Fawkes + gunpowder found.
Guy Fawkes met men at inn. Plotted.	Gunpowder in storeroom under House of Lords.
Guy Fawkes tortured in Tower of London.	1603 James VI of Scotland became James I of England. Protestant. Wanted all to be Protestant
Plotters found lodgings near House of Lords.	

©Hopscotch Educational Publishing

Chapter 1
The Patchwork Quilt, Valerie Flournoy (Puffin, 1985)
From Me to You, Paul Rogers (Orchard, 1987)
Once There Were Giants, Martin Waddell (Walker, 1989)
Grandma's Bill, Jane Johnson, (Macdonald, 1990)

Chapter 2
Linkers: Toys discovered through History, Ken Bryant-Mole
(A & C Black, 1996)

Museums
National Museum of Childhood, Bethnal Green (London)
www.vam.ac.uk/vastatic/nmc/index.html
National Museum of Childhood, Beaumaris, Anglesey
www.nwi.co.uk/museumofchildhood/index.htm
The Teddy Bear Museum, 19 Greenhill Street, Stratford-upon-Avon,
CV37 6LF
www. mailto:info@theteddybearmuseum.com
Museum of Childhood, Edinburgh, 42 High Street, Edinburgh, EH1
1TG http://www.cac.org.uk
London Toy & Model Museum, 21–23 Craven Hill, Bayswater,
London

Chapter 3
Paintings
'Many Happy Returns of the Day', William Frith (Harrogate
Museum & Gallery), 'The Pinch of Poverty', T B Kennington
(Thomas Coram Foundation), 'The Lowther Arcade', H C Bryant
(Coutts & Co), 'Blind Man's Buff', George Goodwin Kilburne (The
Priory Gallery, Cheltenham)

Museums and galleries
The Lady Lever Gallery, Port Sunlight, Cheshire
www.speel.demon.co.uk
Port Sunlight Heritage Centre, Greendale Road, Port Sunlight,
Cheshire

Chapter 5
BBC History http://www.bbc.co.uk/history/
'The Origins of Everyday Things', (Reader's Digest, 1998)

Chapter 6
Mary Seacole, Christine Moorcroft and Magnus Magnusson,
Channel 4 Learning, 1998

Museums
The Florence Nightingale Museum, St Thomas's Hospital, 2
Lambeth Palace Road, London SE1 7EW www.florence-
nightingale.co.uk
National Army Museum, Royal Hospital Road, London SW3 4HT
www.national-army-museum.ac.uk

Science Museum (Wellcome History of Medicine Galleries),
Exhibition Road, London SW7 2DD www.nmsi.ac.uk

Chapter 7
George Stephenson, Christine Moorcroft & Magnus Magnusson,
(Channel 4 Learning, 1998)
Iron Ways, Dinah Starkey & Robert Wilson (Channel 4 Learning,
1996)

Museums
Beamish Open Air Museum, Beamish, DH8 0RG
www.beamish.org.uk
Bowes Railway, Springwell Village, Washington NE9 7QL
www.bowesrailway.co.uk
Darlington Railway Centre and Museum, North Road Station,
Darlington DL3 6ST

Chapter 8
The London Fire Brigade Museum, Winchester House, 94A
Southwark Bridge Road, London SE1 0UG
www.glosc.gov.uk/pubserv/gcc/fire/history/grtfire
www.jmccall.demon.co.uk/history
www.thehistorynet.com/BritishHeritage/articles/1995_text
www.adelpha.com/davidco/History/fire1
www.plus44.co.uk/london44/tour/monument

Chapter 9
The Royal British Legion, 48 Pall Mall London SW1Y 5JY
www.britishlegion.org.uk
For the full text of 'In Flanders Fields' by John McCrae:
www.emory.edu/ENGLISH/LostPoets/McCrae.html
www.fordham.edu/halsall/mod/mccrae-flanders.html
or key into an Internet search 'In Flanders Fields' and several sites
will be displayed.

Chapter 10
Guy Fawkes, Christine Moorcroft & Magnus Magnusson (Channel 4
Learning, 1998)
The Gunpowder Plot, Rhoda Nottridge (Wayland, 1991)
Gunpowder, Treason and Plot, Lewis Winslock (Wayland, 1973)

Museums
Geffrye Museum, Kingsland Road, London E2 8EA
www.geffryemusuem.org.uk
Houses of Parliament, London SW1A 0PW www.parliament.uk
Museum of London, 150 London Wall, London EC2 5HN
www.musuemoflondon.org.uk
Tower of London, London EC3N 4AB www.tower-of-london.com